Praise from Nonprofit Professionals for
Walking the Board Walk

"Vaughn Sherman knows how to 'walk the board walk.' His many years of experience being on boards and conducting board trainings comes through in this handy and practical guide to being an effective board for non-profit organizations."

—Dr. Cindra Smith, author of *Trusteeship in Community Colleges: A Guide to Effective Governance.* Formerly Education Director for the Community College League of California and is now an independent nonprofit board consultant

"Vaughn Sherman understands more about the challenges of board work than anyone else I know. When I encounter a board problem that I've never seen before, I'm likely to turn to Vaughn for advice."

—Gary Davis, PhD, is the former CEO of the Illinois Community College Trustees Association and is now an independent nonprofit board consultant

"When Vaughn told me that he was writing this book, my immediate reaction was, 'Well it's about time.' I had yet to find just the right tool to assist my board members in making the most of their experience. I wanted something to give new and experienced volunteers alike that was inviting and easy to read. I needed it to be short, but packed with the essentials. In *Walking the Board Walk,* I've found what I was looking for and believe that you will too. Whether you are just beginning your board walk or a seasoned director looking to enhance your knowledge base, I wish you the best on your journey!"

—Chris Marx, Executive Director, Edmonds Community College Foundation, Lynnwood, Washington

Walking
The Board Walk

To Jim —
With best wishes —
Vaughn Sherman

Vaughn Sherman

Patos Island Press
Edmonds, Washington

Copyright © 2012, by Vaughn Sherman

Published by
Patos Island Press
705 Spruce Street
Edmonds, Washington 98020
www.patosislandpress.com

Library of Congress Control Number: 2012931674

ISBN: 978-0-9847225-0-1

Printed in the United States of America

Cover image: © Paul Fleet | Fotolia.com
Book and cover design
Jeanie James, Shorebird Media

Table of Contents

Foreword

Board Members

Chief Executive
Officers

Board Members /
CEO Connections

The Board Chair

Talking
the Board Talk

Commitment

Advocacy &
Fundraising

Afterword

Appendices

Author's Notes

Foreword

Why does the book title suggest that nonprofit board work can be enjoyable? Because it *can* and *should be* enjoyable.

The motivation for putting these thoughts together comes from something I've discovered in talking with nonprofit board members who serve boards both large and small—too many are dissatisfied with one or more facets of their volunteer jobs. This small book has been written for anyone involved in nonprofit governance. There are remedies for dissatisfaction and ways to improve board management that I have found in over thirty years of working with scores of nonprofit boards. A great number of nonprofits across the country provide excellent service to their communities, but there are those that fall short in good board management and in offering their board members a rewarding experience. [1]

---

1. For the purposes of this book, the term "board member" is meant to include directors, governors, trustees, and other volunteers who serve non-profit governing boards of institutions, organizations and agencies that operate for the good of their clients. Although there are differences, all are custodians of the governance process.

i

Early in my experience of working with boards, I was included in a Boardwalk program that prepared volunteers as trainers for governing boards of United Way agencies. Those of us who attended the Boardwalk sessions returned to our communities and waited for calls to train boards in the best practices we had learned. When the calls came, they were pleas for help from boards in trouble. It became clear that these boards had not taken time for board training and development. They thought they were doing just fine without that, thank you.

They were doing just fine, that is, until the board began to shrink in numbers because nobody was interested in joining. Or a new executive director was hired, and a personality conflict arose between the director and the board chair. Or the board split four to three on an important issue they couldn't resolve. The list goes on and on, but the point is that those of us trained by Boardwalk were mostly helping boards identify their problems and to rebuild.

In 1981, I received an appointment to a board of trustees that would govern a newly formed community college district. Our college president strongly encouraged us to attend state, regional, and national meetings where we could find training workshops and learn the business of governing community colleges. We were a genial, collegial, effective group serving on that board, an experience that was due not just to a good match of personalities but also, most importantly, to the focus on board education.

Next came participation in the leadership of our state and national community college organizations, and finally a position as a consultant for the national Association of Community College Trustees (ACCT), based in Washington, DC. In this position, I traveled over much of the United States, presenting at workshops and facilitating retreats for many community college boards of trustees. I wrote articles appearing in community college publications, and ACCT published my book, *Essentials of Good Board/CEO Relations.*

Still, for all the workshops, training, and publications offered by ACCT, I found some trustees lacking in the basic skills needed for good board management. As in my local experience, many were asking for help. One of my colleagues agreed with my assessment that too often the problem could have been solved through leadership by a good chairperson.

A valued colleague, Dr. Cindra J. Smith, then Director of Education Services, Community College League of California, joined with me in editing and writing for another ACCT publication: *The Board Chair: A Guide for Leading Community Colleges.* Both publications are highly recommended and available from ACCT at *http://acct.org.*

Fellow consultants have encouraged me to turn these experiences and the information into a more general book on the governance of nonprofit agencies. And this is what you will find in the chapters that follow. This book is not intended to provide a full-scale set of directions for organizing and managing a nonprofit board. Such information is readily available in books and on the Internet, excellent examples being *BoardSource* at *http://boardsource.org* and *All About Boards of Directors* (For Profit and Nonprofit). *http://managementhelp.org/boards/boards.htm.*

This book is intended to help nonprofit board leadership and individuals develop their boards in ways that will improve governance and make the experience more satisfying. Rather than a full set of instructions on how to organize and manage a nonprofit board, I'm covering those areas I've seen as most frequently causing poor board performance and disappointment among individual board members.

If there is one critical theme that I'd like to stress as you open these pages, it's the importance of how we listen to our fellow board members and how we talk to them. These are at the heart of good communications, for without good communications the technical matters of governance cannot be applied with excellence.

If there is one critical theme that I'd like to stress as you open these pages, it's the importance of how we listen to our fellow board members and how we talk to them. These are at the heart of good communications, for without good communications the technical matters of governance cannot be applied with excellence.

Board Members

RECRUITMENT, ORIENTATION, MENTORING, DEPARTURE

> ❝ *My definition of a team is one in which the whole is greater than the sum of the parts. Otherwise, it is just a collection of individuals. I find it impossible to imagine how my definition can be achieved if the team is comprised of clones of a single individual—no matter how good that individual is. Making the whole greater than the sum of the parts is about exploiting the differences between people, not the similarities.* ❞
>
> – Alan Hunt, in an article posted on
> SA Business Hub, April 2, 2006,
> *www.sabusinesshub.co.za/*

Recruitment

In preparing for the recruitment of board members, it's important to keep in mind what it means to be a member of the current board. How might a candidate fit in? Later in the book, we'll discuss some of the nuts and bolts, rules and regulations of being a board member. When considering a candidate's potential to work comfortably under those rules, it's important to look at what kind of team player he or she might be within this group. How will the candidate deal with the fact that a board is made up of individual members, but its authority comes from acting as one body? No single member—not even the chairperson—can act alone with authority on policy or related matters. If your candidate has a reputation as a cowboy (in the reckless sense), consider him/her carefully before keeping that person on the list.

A good nonprofit board can be seen as a cast of several role players, each unique in their skills, life experiences, and community connections brought to the table. This need for diversity is one of several matters needing discussion when a board organizes or reaches out for new members.

I've worked with boards lacking in one or more areas of diversity (racial, gender, professional backgrounds, political affiliations, community contacts, etc.). A few years ago, I facilitated a retreat for a board of twelve people seriously lacking in diversity. They were well mixed in professional backgrounds, but only one of the twelve was a woman and there was no racial diversity on an all white board in a state with a significant minority population. They rejected my suggestion of setting a goal to increase board diversity.

Several years after the retreat, that board appears to have much the same composition. This is an example of the fact that many nonprofit boards are self-perpetuating; the board members seek out replacements for those leaving the board. In practice they tend to recruit people like themselves. As with any organized activity, boards have their own cultures and culture is famously hard to change. Thus a fine board tends to renew its excellence when bringing on new members, while a less functional board leans towards retaining its weaknesses.

Does your board need to replace a member or add one or more new members? To begin the process, a decision must be made to determine those who will be responsible for the search. On a small board, it may be most practical to involve the board as a whole. On a larger board, it might be appropriate for a standing committee or an ad hoc committee chosen solely for this one purpose, or played even closer to the vest with a single individual authorized to handle the entire process.

The first duty of the responsible body is to identify

what kind of board member is needed. Too often the answer is someone you're quite sure will say yes—a friend, a known and respected community member with experience on other boards, or someone who gets a lot of press in the area and seems a likely candidate to attract attention to the organization, to be a figurehead. Unless they have the solid qualifications needed, none of these is a good choice by simply relying upon those definitions. An early task must be identifying the profile for the type of new board member who is best able to advance the work of the board.

Keeping in mind the need for maintaining diversity, people with skills in the law might be considered if an attorney is being replaced and there are no others on the board. If the board is under expansion to become a fundraising organization—as is happening frequently in today's world—thought should be given to including people with money or with ready access to people with money. The latter might be bankers, accountants, investment brokers, or others with similar backgrounds and contacts in the community. What are the racial demographics of the area served, and how well does your board mirror them? Other diversity matters call for candidates with a variety of social and business contacts, and anything else that might best serve board effectiveness and the mission of the organization.

It must be noted that there are many governmental agencies that operate without profit and fit the profile of nonprofit leadership covered here. Far too numerous to list here, they include agencies with missions in health, education, social services, agriculture, utilities, and a host of others. They may operate with boards whose directors or trustees are elected or are appointed by officials like state governors, county executive officers, county commissioners, etc. Many of these boards consider it inappropriate to influence the selection process, whether through election or appointment. On the other hand, I know of elected boards that encourage the candidacy of individuals considered as good prospects, and some appointed boards that regularly inform their appointing authorities about people who would be a good fit for their governance style. If a board intends to begin this kind of influence, it would be prudent to check on the legalities before taking that course of action.

Next, the entire board must be involved through presentation of the list of candidates to all members. At this point directors will review suggestions made by the nominating group, and may be able to add information about those with whom they are acquainted.

Nonprofit boards are so varied in character that there is no single best method for approaching candidates. Generally speaking a first contact should be made by the board member who has suggested the candidate, accompanied by the executive director or another board member. These representatives should make it clear that the purpose of the meeting is to get an understanding as to possible interest the candidate might have in serving on the board. This is also an opportunity for an assessment by someone in addition to the person who proposed the candidate.

For boards that have identified many possible candidates it may be best not to make a commitment to the candidate at this point; there could be more candidates than open board positions. In this case the results of the first meeting will be brought back for comparison with other candidate interviews, followed by an approach to the person identified by the board committee as the top candidate selected. In smaller communities with a more limited slate of candidates, the first meeting may be the best chance to nail down a candidate's agreement to serve on the board.

Whichever step of those outlined above is followed, it's essential that the chosen candidate be completely aware of the responsibilities he or she is accepting in an agreement to join the board.

- What is the frequency of board meetings? Where are they held?
- What are the meeting times, and how long do they last?

- How many hours a week is a board member expected to devote to the board and the organization it represents?
- Is there a financial obligation to donate to the organization?

A written document outlining answers to these questions and more should be provided before the candidate signs on the dotted line. (See Appendix A for an example)

The final stage of recruitment may require board approval to accept the new member into the fold. The organization's bylaws will direct action needed to officially seat a new director.

Orientation

There is widespread opinion that it takes about a year for a new member to become effective on a nonprofit board. For some of the more complicated organizations with boards such as those in education and health care, the learning curve may be considered as long as three years. Clearly, a new board member needs to be as well prepared as possible to deal with elements of activity that are unfamiliar.

Orientation should be undertaken seriously by board leadership. The executive director—and perhaps other staff members in the case of a large organization—must be involved along with selected board members and appropriate committees. Orientation should occur as soon as possible after recruitment, and include at least the following topics:

- Board history and mission
- The relationship between the board and the organization served
- Details regarding the organization
- Policy review
- Role of the board
- Individual board member responsibilities
- Staff roles, relationship to the board
- Committee assignments

Members of small boards may find such a list overwhelming. This does not absolve them from orienting new members at whatever level is appropriate to the size and charter of their board and the organization served.

Mentoring

However experienced a new board member might be in nonprofit board work, the previous service will not translate directly to taking part in the governance of a new organization. There is much to be learned about the new board. No matter how thorough an orientation might be, there are nuances of board operations and relationships that can best be learned from someone who already knows the ins and outs of membership on this board.

The use of mentors for new board members is too often overlooked. Advantages of mentoring new members are many, including: bringing them more quickly up to speed in their roles; good member retention; and, over time, adding to the spirit of board members' camaraderie.

Matching an experienced board member with a newcomer to the board is important. Beyond advantages of similar backgrounds and interests, there's an advantage to selecting mentors who are the most committed among board members. A high level of commitment apparent in a mentor can add enthusiasm as the newcomer learns the routines of serving on the board.

A mentor's role usually lasts for the first year of a new member's time on the board. The mentor's responsibilities should not be too time-consuming: an initial meeting with the mentee over lunch or coffee, calling before board meetings to assure that the new member understands the agenda and is given answers to questions he or she might have, and perhaps a few other calls or brief meetings during the year as needed.

Departing

There are a number of reasons for members leaving their boards. Term limits for board membership are common, sometimes there are limits placed on the number of terms one can serve. Three- to five-year terms on a board are common, while term limits seem to be more varied. While many boards have no term limits, many do have limits of two or three terms.

Problems can arise when an especially capable or popular board member reaches the end of her or his term limit. Everyone wants to see the person stay on the board, bringing temptation to fudge the issue. Such a temptation should be resisted. The only ethical way of avoiding this member's departure is to change the policy regarding term limits, allowing a longer time on the board. That might be fine for this one instance, but the other side of the coin is a situation where an inefficient or unpleasant member has an opportunity to remain longer than other board members might wish. The solution is a regular review of the policy to assure that it best serves the board's governance, and to stick with policy once it's set.

Some boards have policies covering reasons for dismissal of a board member. In addition to various malfeasance issues, the most common I've seen relates to attendance at board meetings. And the most common among those is that a board member may be dismissed for three or more unexcused absences during the calendar year.

Board members also depart voluntarily for personal reasons such as a move to another city, health or family problems, or an increase in time demands. Such departures should be accepted graciously.

A different kind of response deals with the need to dismiss a board member for cause other than what might appear in the bylaws. This is truly a tough problem. I've seen such issues as a board member calling a press conference to reveal the proceedings of an executive session; regular use of foul, inappropriate language during board meetings; total and flagrant disregard of board policy regarding sensitive minority issues; and more. They put me in mind of a particularly adventurous son who I scolded at age six for dropping water balloons on pedestrians, two stories below our hotel room. "You never told me not to do that," he sobbed. You can never think of all the things an imaginative young boy should not do, just as there is no complete list I could offer of outrageous behavior some board members might demonstrate.

What can a board do in such a case? The first action must be taken by the board chair, who needs to communicate concern about the inappropriate action directly with the offending board member. This can be done in a number of ways, but my preference is a meeting called by the board chair, away from any venue tied to the organization. Getting together in a coffee shop or a restaurant lessens the inevitable tension rising from what the offending board member will rightly see as a scolding.

If the board member continues to exhibit unacceptable behavior, it seems fair to give them a second, sterner warning in a less friendly venue. Public censure during a board meeting is the next step, but in my experience the offending party is so dug into position by this time that it doesn't seem to make much difference. If that doesn't work and the case is serious enough to damage the reputation of board and organization, it's probably time to talk to an attorney. The range of possibilities for action is limitless, and varies greatly from state to state. Appointed board members may have their appointments withdrawn, while recall elections might be possible in some areas, but there are cases where these aren't possible.

The way to avoid messy situations like these is to go back to the beginning of this chapter; i.e., taking care about recruitment of board members.

*The Board and
the Chief Executive Officer*

BEGINNING—DEPARTING

Beginning

It's hard to think of a single matter more critical to good board relations with a chief executive officer (CEO) than being able to rely on the complete integrity of each board member, the board as a whole, and the CEO. Little can affect us negatively in community standing if we have a united leadership that embodies truly ethical behavior, shows staff, clients, and community that they are dealing with a leadership grounded in integrity and good ethical principles. Whether it is the simple appointment of a board member of a small board to serve as volunteer manager, or a national search for the CEO of a large organization, the board demonstrates its integrity in properly seeking a good match to the organization and governance style in any candidate it selects.

Challenges for managing a small organization without an executive director center on which board member has the talent and experience needed to carry out the management responsibilities. The activists who volunteer for board duty are usually busy people, which can make it difficult to find someone who has the skills and time beyond work and family for taking on management of the organization. Whatever the situation for this kind of organization, board leadership needs to be careful not to passively accept a board member as manager. The job is too important. It's worth taking the time and making the effort to get the best possible person into the position.

Challenges for a larger board looking for a salaried CEO are different. Depending on the size and mission of the organization, decisions must be made regarding the scope of the search. Will the board and staff conduct the search, or hire a specialized company to do the work? An important decision will be the preparation and approval of an announcement about the position opening. The board is responsible for assuring that the presentation honestly portrays the current situation of the organization.

There is much to discuss when putting together a job description for a new CEO. Reviewing and making necessary revisions to the CEO's job description will be one area of discussion, along with compensation that might be offered, educational requirements such as whether or not to require a particular education degree, what form of contract will be offered, and many others. This is only the beginning of an exhaustive list that should be discussed before a job announcement is made public. If the current CEO's departure is a friendly turnover, he or she can help with details involved in preparing for the search for a successor. In this case, it must be made clear to all that the departing CEO has no involvement in the selection itself.

Just as with the hiring board, candidates for a chief executive officer position need to demonstrate solid integrity, presenting themselves with honesty about their abilities and experience. There is a temptation to inflate these in order to secure a position, to use friendships inappropriately, or to gloss over the less successful parts of a career. These are temptations that must be resisted, as anything less than honesty in this regard can come back to haunt the relationship.

No matter the size of your board, the appointment or hiring of a new CEO brings a wonderful opportunity.

Chief Executive Officer

This is a time when course correction is possible, a time to review board policy delegating responsibilities to the CEO, and a time to review the passing relationship for improvements that can be made in connecting with the CEO. In short, it's a time for building towards even greater success.

Departing

An executive director's length of time in office is dependent on performance in managing an organization, as measured against policy that delegates responsibilities of the position. This is usually set out in a contract that can range in formality from a handshake deal to a written document pored over by attorneys for the organization and the prospective CEO. The contracts can take many forms, most with a time limit and many with a "rollover" provision that allows automatic renewal if performance is satisfactory.

As with board directors, many different scenarios can bring an end to the tenure of an executive director. Whether it's retirement, desired job change, a failure of the board to renew a contract, or an outright termination for cause, there is always some stress involved. As a board member I've personally gone through termination for cause of the much-admired CEO of a large institution. The result of an ethics violation, the severity left no recourse but termination. It was a terrible experience not only for those of us involved in governance, but for staff and clients of the organization as well. And it was a lesson about the importance of practicing good ethics by everyone involved in the leadership of nonprofits.

Good boardsmanship can be sorely tried when considering termination of a CEO for reasons other than a voluntary departure. Clear-cut cases like the one mentioned above, which was widely reported by the media, might unite the board. But performance seen by a board majority as marginal, leading to non-renewal of contract, can split a board and lead to hard feelings all around. I've seen some splits resulting from bitter disputes over a CEO's dismissal. Years ago I was called by the chair to lead a board retreat for a large nonprofit organization, and given the idea that the board was unanimous in a decision for non-renewal of the executive director's contract. Between the agreement for the mediation and the time I arrived for the retreat, the situation had changed so completely that the board was in a five/four split and the outgoing CEO refused to talk with me, even by telephone. Facilitation of that retreat was a real challenge.

Chief Executive Officer

How do we avoid such situations? The answer is the same as mentioned previously in the case of dismissing board directors: *go back to the beginning of the chapter.*

A careful search process committed to choosing an executive director who will best fit management needs for the organization, followed by excellent communications between the board and the CEO, will go a long way towards prevention of this kind of trouble.

Notes

_____

_____

_____

_____

_____

_____

_____

_____

_____

_____

_____

_____

Board / CEO Connections

RELATING, RESPONSIBILITIES, COMMUNICATING

Relating

One of the most important understandings between the CEO and the board regards their separate responsibilities. This would seem to be a simple matter, but misunderstandings about their different jobs are often at the heart of serious problems in governance.

Who does what? How do you know? For boards and CEOs at the beginning of a relationship, the answer truly is simple; they must talk to each other. These partners in leadership need to meet early in the relationship, devoting time for discussion and reaching agreement about their separate responsibilities. The meeting is best held as a retreat soon after hiring. It could include presentations by staff or other information items of mutual interest to the board and CEO. In this case, two or three hours of the retreat should be devoted to a board-CEO private session discussing the new relationship, including their separate roles and responsibilities and other matters between the partners. It's important to get an early agreement about communications between the board and CEO, including who communicates, how often, and in what manner.

Leadership of smaller organizations may simplify the means, but it's as imperative for them as it is for those in larger bodies that there is a clear understanding regarding the separate jobs of the board and whoever takes on the management role.

Boards of the kind discussed here are policy-making bodies that delegate day-to-day management of the institution to the CEO, or to a business manager or specific board member for some smaller boards. This separation of functions between management and governance needs to permeate the understanding of all parties involved.

One of my early mentors advised, "board members keep their noses in and their hands out of matters concerning management." This is excellent advice, but there is a caveat: small boards without executive directors may need to use their members for various management duties. In such cases, the classic separation of policy and administration is overridden by the situation.

Nonprofit boards should take the greatest care in delegating responsibilities, and in seeing to it that the board and its individual members do not violate agreements with the CEO. One of the major irritants in the board-CEO relationship is micromanagement. In the governance sense, micromanagement occurs when board members—or the board as a whole—interfere with management issues that have been delegated to the CEO. Administrative leaders are understandably sensitive about incursions into their territory.

Board Members and CEOs

By the same token, CEOs at times yield to temptations that draw them into their board's governance responsibilities. An example might be the CEO taking action on a matter that requires board approval. Unless a board is well-educated and has a good backbone for keeping a proper relationship with the CEO, it's too easy to let such invasions pass.

One means for assisting in the relationship is for boards and their CEOs to encourage each other in professional development. There are many conferences and workshops sponsored by national and state nonprofit organizations, some tailored for board members, some for executive directors, and some for both. Continuing education of both is one of the best ways of guaranteeing a well-functioning leadership.

Responsibilities

So, what are the separate responsibilities of the chief executive and the board? There is a wide range of large and small nonprofits with a variety of service goals, but here are some responsibilities that are common:

» CEO Responsibilities

Typically, all duties of management are delegated to the CEO, with occasional exceptions left to the board. An example might be board involvement in hiring at top levels of the executive, or board approval of the CEO's decision on such hirings. One common exception is a limit on expensive purchases, such as a requirement for board approval on purchases exceeding an amount appropriate to the organization.

» Board Responsibilities

Responsibilities of the board of directors are not always well understood. There is a notion in some circles that board members don't have much to do after hiring a CEO until it's time to let him or her go. Many years ago I heard a board member suggest that board meetings be held only once every six months, with a single agenda item—should the CEO be fired? If the answer is no, everyone goes out for a good dinner. If it's *yes,* board members roll up their sleeves and go to work hiring a new chief executive officer.

Of course that was in jest, but it echoes a problem—some board members do not understand what is expected of the board. For a technical discussion of this matter, one of the experts is John Carver. Carver has developed *Policy Governance®*, a methodology for developing policies and delineating the separate roles of CEO and board. His program has been adopted by many nonprofits across the country, and his ideas have influenced other boards. His web site, Carver Governance Design, Inc, at *www. carvergovernance.com,* provides details.

Board Members and CEOs

Nonprofit boards have in common several responsibilities beyond developing policy:

- *Links to the Community*—Board members, whether appointed, elected, or simply chosen by their peers on the board, represent the community to the organization, and the organization back to the community. They are in a position to understand local needs and how the organization can best serve those needs. This is the way the vision for the organization's future is formed. All board members need to understand the process, and the board needs to set aside discussion time to encourage members to share their ideas.

- *Monitoring*—The board needs a process for measuring the effectiveness of the organization, best done through checking performance against goals and objectives. To be fair and effective, the goals and objectives must be agreed upon in advance by the CEO and the board when developing a monitoring system.

- *Evaluating*—Monitoring provides benchmarks that are useful in evaluating the CEO's performance. These evaluations should be made at regular intervals, at least annually. The board would be well-advised to evaluate its own performance as well. The form the self-evaluations take will depend on the size of the institution and resources available to the board, but at the very least there should be a focused conversation about their own effectiveness in governing. (See Appendices B and C for more information and samples).

- *Fiscal Responsibility*—Financial health of the organization is a concern of the board, as demonstrated through the approval of annual budgets, scheduled monitoring of spending vs. revenues, and long-range planning. Many boards are directly involved in fundraising to sustain the organization or to supplement other monies that are part of the income stream.

This is not in any way intended to be an exhaustive list of board duties, but only to introduce some that are common to many nonprofit boards. An important point on which to end this discussion: the more a board stays busy by properly focusing on its governance responsibilities, the less chance that the board and its members will delve into managerial territory belonging to the CEO.

Board Members and CEOs

» **Communicating**

It's hard to overstate the importance of good communications between the board and CEO, and among the board members. As mentioned in the introduction of this book, without good communications the technical matters of governance cannot be applied with excellence.

My perception of good communications between board and chief executive officer is an easy, open, comfortable flow back and forth with no doubts on anyone's part that they are hearing full, factual, and useful information. In my experience with troubled boards, it's the "full" part that is often missing. Among the causes is the intentional omission of facts because they might be embarrassing to one or more parties, or the facts simply aren't understood as pertinent to the discussion. And all too often the problem is just a lack of good communications between and among the parties due to poor management of the board relationship.

We've seen a recent example in the case of a superintendant dismissed by a large school district over fraud in one area of her administration. It wasn't "the buck stops at the top" that brought her dismissal. Rather, it was her failure to keep the board informed of growing signs of fraud prior to the audit that led to discovery of the problem—an excellent example of the need to report fully.

What should be communicated? The details for any one nonprofit must be worked out by the concerned parties, in venues such as a retreat or other opportunities for discussions between board and CEO. As manager of an enterprise, the CEO keeps the board informed of successes and problems, concerns and kudos regarding his personnel, and much more. Sometimes there is so much to report that board members feel overwhelmed by the information. Striking a balance between how much information is available for distribution by the CEO and how much is appropriate to board member duties should be part of the discussions among these leaders. Finding the proper balance can be critical to success not only of the CEO-board relationship, but to the endeavors of the organization itself.

The range of discussions between board and CEO

should be clear in the delegation of duties and other policies. If the board governs a large organization there will be reporting from the CEO on events and progress of the organization. Staff members sometime accompany the CEO to monthly board meetings to round out reporting that touches on their areas of responsibility. The scope and detail change with diminishing size of the nonprofit, but not the need to keep the board fully informed of all matters affecting governance.

Board Members and CEOs

Friendships are wonderful. If we haven't been friends with new board members before they are recruited, friendships are often developed on the board. This is good, but care needs to be taken not to form cliques that result in the board splitting over an issue. It's sometimes said that CEOs should not have friendships with board members. That's pretty extreme, but the CEO must at least use care in disseminating information about management and the institution even-handedly to board members. I've seen board members furious because they found other members privy to information not given to them.

Those involved in governance need to follow the "no surprise rule." A CEO does not like to hear that the board has been planning an action without her or his knowledge. As noted above, a board does not like to learn of fraud after an exception to the audit. The no surprise rule is at the heart of open communications.

The atmosphere surrounding exchanges of information will be considered later in chapters entitled "The Board Chair" and "Talking the Talk."

> *Let it be said again: good communications are critical to the success of the board-CEO relationship, to the satisfactory experience of all involved, and to the progress of the organization itself.*

Notes

_____

_____

_____

_____

_____

_____

_____

_____

_____

_____

_____

The Board Chair

Choosing, Running Effective Meetings,
Rules Of Procedure

Choosing

"Chairman of the Board" is a title that has a sense of honor and respect, especially when applied to entertainment figures or those who govern major corporations. It's a shame that volunteers who serve on nonprofit boards don't always give the position the same respect when choosing their leaders, with proper thought given to that person's availability, training, and preparation for the job. When deciding upon a new chair, I've heard board members suggest another member who was not present at the meeting, since that person could not object. Even in jest it suggests a cavalier attitude about what is the most important job in the governance of a nonprofit organization.

To better understand why the position of board chair should be so respected, let's look at the chair's responsibilities. The board chair:

- Maintains a special relationship with the CEO, vital to effective governance of the institution. In this capacity the board chair meets separately with the CEO, developing meeting agendas, representing the board's ideas, concerns and other matters needing discussion. He or she also acts as a sounding board, allowing the CEO to discuss matters before taking them to the full board.

- Is spokesperson for the board of directors. The chair is usually the designated person to speak with the media on anything related to board business, unless the board has taken action to choose another director to act as spokesperson.

- "Owns" the agenda for board meetings. Though the CEO should be involved in preparing the agenda, the chair directs meetings and thus carries ultimate responsibility for its contents and presentation.

- Is responsible for smoothly conducting board

meetings in a way that is fair to all participants.

- Serves as the chief reference and facilitator for all board matters both in and out of business sessions.

This kind of description for a board chair's responsibilities suggests much work, many skills, and a lot of knowledge and experience needed by those willing to accept the position, among them:

- A thorough knowledge of governing policies developed by the board.
- Good understanding of Roberts Rules of Order, or another set of rules used in conducting board meetings.
- An ability to facilitate exchanges and conversations among trustees, both in and out of the board meeting room.
- An involvement in the community that promotes interaction between the board and the community.

There are several ways nonprofit board chairs are selected, including appointments by higher authority for some government-funded institutions, membership election, a choice made by the board itself, or even annual rotation of board members. Whatever the method used, an institution will be better served by a board that is serious about its top leadership.

Conducting Meetings

When I hear complaints from people serving on nonprofit boards, many have to do with board meetings. They start too late, run too long, the agenda isn't followed, there's too much idle chatter instead of discussion of board business. There are many ways in which a board chair can smooth the proceedings of a meeting so that participants find them pleasant and productive. Some of them are considered here.

» A welcoming atmosphere

When we walk into a group meeting of any kind, there are first impressions important to our anticipation about the event. One of those is connected with the surroundings. Are they reasonably comfortable and quiet enough for discussion? The chair and CEO need to work together to choose a venue appropriate to the board.

A welcoming atmosphere also includes greetings from the host, just as in a party at home. In this case the chair is host. Chairpersons should make an effort to greet all board members as they arrive, and to introduce guests as one of the first items of business.

» Starting on Time

One of the chief complaints about board meetings is the chair's failure to start the meeting on time. And it's the easiest to correct. I think the tendency to delay opening a meeting is often due to a chair's fear that the late parties' feelings will be hurt if the group doesn't wait for their arrival.

The problem with waiting for latecomers is twofold. The first and most obvious issue is that a board chair waiting for latecomers is wasting the time of busy board members, staff, and guests who are courteous enough to arrive on time. The second issue is that by doing so, chronic latecomers will be encouraged to continue their bad habits.

The board chair who regularly starts scheduled meetings on time will find participants and the audience getting the message rather quickly. Responsible board members will not want to be seen missing part of the meetings, nor will the CEO and staff want to be viewed as negligent in this way.

It's understandable that a chair might want to wait for a quorum before starting the proceedings, especially if there's an early action item such as approval of a consent agenda. I hope a chair will have the courage to reflect in the minutes the late arrival of any members who are chronically late. Someone who is late because of transportation or family problems might be excused. The chair needs to remind board members who are chronically late that their behavior is not acceptable.

The Board Chair

» Setting a Positive Tone

The gavel bangs the table. The chair is about to start the meeting. Even if there is no agenda item for welcome and greetings, this is a critical time for setting a good tone for the meeting, an opportune moment to greet everyone and help them feel comfortable. With informal remarks before taking up the business at hand, the chair can put the group into a pleasant frame of mind.

Studies of group behavior have shown that creating an expectation of good things to come at the beginning of a meeting helps the proceedings that follow. Even having small gifts at each board seat can enhance the conversational flow. It isn't very practical for a board chair to arrange material gifts for those attending a meeting, but the chair can give verbal gifts of positive comments and good will that help provide the expectation of good things to come.

» Preparing the Agenda

The agenda is an important tool for board chairs to use as they direct proceedings at board meetings. It follows that the chair plays a crucial part in the development of that tool.

For smaller nonprofits without an executive director, the chair doesn't have much choice but to be the person putting the agenda together. With an executive director, the formality of a relationship with the board chair increases with the size of the institution. So, too, does the executive officer's involvement in agenda building. Thus, in larger organizations, the board chair and CEO need to schedule a meeting aimed at agreeing on an agenda for the next board meeting.

It can be seen from the above that in larger organizations the board chair may be tempted to leave agenda development mostly to the CEO. Bending to that temptation is a mistake. The meeting and its proceedings belong to the chair. The board meeting is where governance is practiced, not executive direction. The CEO has every right, has in fact the responsibility to place items on the agenda affecting management of the institution. But this must be done in close collaboration with the board of directors through the board chair.

» Conducting the Flow of Business

Poorly conducted meetings are among the things that disturb nonprofit board members. One of my sons has accused me of being power hungry because I've risen to the top leadership in several organizations. I'd like to think that he was joking, but in my defense I don't enjoy serving on boards with meetings that start late, are full of unproductive chatter, and poorly conducted in general. By running them myself, I can control the proceedings and save myself a lot of aggravation.

And this is a good place to suggest to readers a way to improve your skills beyond relying on training and books: make careful observation of fellow board members and board chairs who demonstrate good skills in meetings, who demonstrate good boardsmanship. Watching skilled executive directors can also be useful. In addition to my formal training, I can think of two people who most influenced my abilities in board work. One was a fellow board member of ACCT who eventually rose to the presidency of that organization, and the other was an executive director of a United Way agency. The former had great skills in directing meetings; the executive director also had those skills and shared them with me as a mentor when I was tapped to serve as board chair for the agency.

» Rules of Procedure

There seems to be a knee-jerk reaction when a group formally organizes and learns that an approving authority will require the organization to include rules of procedure in its authorizing documents. Oftentimes the reaction is "Oh yes, we know Robert's rules so lets put that in our policy." The book of Robert's Rules was first published in 1876 with the intention of finding some kind of standard for conducting meeting of societies, and was based mostly on parliamentary procedure as practiced in the United States Congress. The tenth edition is currently referenced, and titled Robert's Rules of Procedure Newly Revised.

This valuable, venerable tool is the most commonly used parliamentary procedure in the United States, but it is not recognized by the courts as rising to the level of the law. There are several alternatives, the most used of these being The Standard Code of Parliamentary Procedure. It is important to underscore that the board of an organization registering with the state is required to have procedural rules for its meetings. Whatever set of rules best fits the needs of that board is written into the bylaws, including rules adopted by the board. Boards establishing rules of procedure or adopting new rules need to consult laws of their states, but generally it is required that the rules allow for effective and fair conduct of business.

People rightly have great respect for the genius of Robert's rules and for board members who have a thorough knowledge of their organizations' rules and how to apply them. It truly is a blessing to have a knowledgeable board chair who leads a meeting in such a way that all members can be certain they will be recognized and be able to take part in the conduct of business. But for many of the boards considered here, a very strict use of rules can stifle creative conversation about the business at hand.

This leads me to think what it would be like if NFL regulations were applied to a sandlot football game. It could be done, but the game would last much longer and the kids would have much less fun than if they just did what they usually do: make up their own rules.

One means of allowing creative conversation during board meetings is the use of Robert's Rules for small boards. If your board doesn't have more than a dozen members present at meetings, you should know that Robert's Rules has a special procedure for small boards that takes away much of the formality necessary in large assemblies. Some examples of the small board rules are:

- Members are not required to obtain the floor before making motions or speaking.
- Motions don't need to be seconded.
- There is no limit to the number of times a member can speak to a question.
- Informal discussion of a subject is permitted while no motion is pending.
- When a proposal is clear to all present, a vote can be taken without a motion having been introduced.

The above is only a sketch of the complete rules for small boards. Clearly this procedure is more conducive to creative conversation than following the *Robert's Rules* intended for large assemblies.

A *note of caution:* As mentioned above, a change in the rules must be a matter of policy reflected in the bylaws or other appropriate authorizing documents. Chairpersons using small board rules should become thoroughly familiar with the rules as they appear in Robert's Rules of Order Newly Revised.

Notes

Notes

Talking the Board Talk

All of the preceding suggestions are important to the smooth operation of a nonprofit's leadership team. It is possible, though, to have all of them in place and still suffer from a fragmented, poorly functioning leadership. When this happens, personality conflicts and the lack of a facilitating board process are often at the heart of the problem.

Board process is usually thought of as following the set of written rules that guide operations of the board. They may include policies on conduct, planning cycles, officers, a set of bylaws and more. *The Policy Governance®* method encourages boards to write down and follow whatever practices they have. In doing so it helps boards to codify their practices, and often helps improve existing policies.

But we're talking here about a different kind of process, one that involves respect among board members, between the board and president, and toward staff and stakeholders. According to Roger M. Schwartz, author of *The Skilled Facilitator:*

❝ *Process refers to how a group works together. Process includes how members talk to each other, how they identify and solve problems, how they make decisions, and how they handle conflict.* **❞**

It's this definition of process that we're considering. Communicating, problem solving, decision-making, and conflict resolution are important to what actually happens on a board, no matter the method chosen for governance. We can begin an understanding of this kind of process by looking at the variety of skills and abilities needed by a facilitator. Among others, they include:

- active listening
- observing
- remembering behavior and conversation
- communicating clearly
- acting as a model of good boardsmanship
- openly accepting feedback
- an ability to paraphrase what others have said
- monitoring and changing one's own behavior when necessary

Although a board chair directs the flow of business during meetings, members share a responsibility for conducting business smoothly. If all members acted with these skills and abilities in mind, there would be little chance of problems involved with the business of governance as practiced at board meetings.

Dealing with Difficult Behavior

Joseph W. Duffy is a Seattle attorney who specializes in dispute resolution, including arbitration, mediation, and facilitation. He believes that counterproductive behavior on boards is often due to intrapersonal conflict that originates in the emotional and psychological makeup of a person and is usually not recognized by other members of the group.

According to Duffy's ideas, intrapersonal conflict can be caused by an individual's concerns about his or her role, or power position, in a group. The resulting behavior may include veering from the subject at hand, dominating conversation, withdrawing into silence, attacking the chairperson, or playing the role of expert. He describes this kind of behavior as power seeking, as the individual places a higher priority on personal recognition than on the group's task.

The challenge for groups is to find a way to mitigate the intrapersonal conflicts of difficult members by addressing the overt behavior. Duffy notes that research supports the idea that when group members understand and accept their roles and see the group as mutually supportive, the group produces better, more substantive results. He suggests the following approaches to reducing power seeking behavior and enhancing group effectiveness:

- Training people to become effective board members;
- Creating opportunities for members to become better acquainted with each other;
- Helping people recognize that service as a board member may involve assuming a new and different role;
- Bringing in a facilitator to help identify patterns of disruption;
- Letting members know the effect of disruptive behavior on the group, thus allowing them to change, and;
- Paying attention to process—for example, starting meetings on time and following the agenda.

Some years ago my wife attended a seminar entitled "Dealing with Difficult People." I was struck by one seminar conclusion that she shared with me: there is no such thing as a difficult person, only people whose needs have not been met. The theory is that if you can identify and meet those needs, the other person will no longer be difficult. I've practiced that idea in a number of situations both professional and personal, with enough success that I believe it's worthwhile considering when you come up against someone who seems hard to get along with in the board setting.

My first attempt was personal. Playing at a duplicate bridge center we encountered Daisy, an older woman who had outrageously bad behavior at the bridge table, most of all towards her partner, the unfortunate husband. Why he accepted her abuse was hard to understand, and everybody dreaded a move to their table. Thinking about the difficult people theory, I told my wife: "Just watch. I'll have her eating out of my hand in a month's time." A bold statement, but I was about to experiment.

Our second experience with Daisy started out as badly as the first, but I found out something about her. When I asked about her background, I learned that she had been a beauty queen. She preened a bit when telling me this, so it gave me an idea. On our next dreaded turn at Daisy's table, I began by complimenting her on her dress, wondering where a person could buy a dress like that. She ate it up, and was measurably nicer for that round. The following week I was really impressed with her hairdo, and the week after that with something else.

I was wrong in what I told my wife, because it took more like a couple of months to bring Daisy around. By that time she was trying to make eye contact with me even before we got to her table, and almost giddy when we were there. It's easy to see how this experience also fits in with Duffy's theories. Instead of just being angry and disgusted about difficult behavior, the best approach is an effort to find out what's behind the offending person's actions. If that's successful it may be possible to go some distance towards settling the needs that were discovered. But not always.

I've worked with a couple of boards, and know of others, where the motivation of the offending party is known but there's nothing anyone can do about it. Both situations involved elected board members who for whatever reasons continued to be re-elected against the wishes of the board, the organization, and larger district served. Sometimes, again not always, it's possible to have an appointing authority pull back an appointment, or to have a recall election. If neither is possible, the board can isolate the offending member, or in extreme cases vote for censure. I can't think of a more challenging situation than having to deal with a board member who ignores policies and board culture, and yet cannot be dislodged from his or her position. In one of these cases, the executive director resigned in favor of joining a more reasonably governed organization.

Leading a retreat for another board, I learned that in one of their public meetings, with a journalist present, one of the board members used the "n" word disparagingly about an African-American group connected with the institution. And this occurred with an African-American woman attending as a member of the board, highly qualified and a fine board member. The chair failed to call him on that egregious use of the language, which in part led to the invitation for my facilitation of a board retreat. It will be no surprise that I spent much retreat time talking about the responsibility of chairpersons. I understand that things are going better there now.

This puts me in mind of my own case of posing a challenge for a board I served as an ordinary member. In discussions having to do with a financial situation during a regular board meeting, with staff present, I suggested to the executive director that his solution to the problem was "niggardly." In a private meeting after that, the CEO told me that an African-American staff member complained about my use of that word. Together we looked up the meaning of the word (stingy, miserly), and though we found no relationship to the "n" word, I'll never again use it in public.

Perception trumps fact almost every time.

Successful Boards

We can get more insight into the board process by thinking about the characteristics of a successful board, one known to function well. Experts on behavior refer to this as a mature group, and have concluded that the following contribute to group effectiveness:

» Involvement

Members feel a sense of ownership for the success of the board. The chairperson has special functions to perform, but addressing group difficulties becomes everyone's concern.

» Responsibility

Members assume responsibility for their own behavior and its effect on the task and on their relationship with other group members.

» Trust and Caring

Members trust and care about one another enough to openly express their concerns and feelings. They have also learned how to learn from each other.

» Use of Resources

Diversity of viewpoints is expected and encouraged. The contributions of all group members are sought, valued, and put to use.

» Listening

Members actively listen to one another, which means listening for and communicating understanding. It's more than simply waiting one's turn to talk.

» Self-Examination

The group is willing to examine its own processes. When it is functioning well the group can turn from task orientation to an examination of process issues.

How does your board measure up to these characteristics? Boards that do measure up should celebrate and reinforce their successes. Board members whose boards fall short should take action to help resolve their problems. A leadership evaluation is a good place to start. This is a combination of using the evaluations for both CEO and board mentioned earlier, and holding a private session with both parties to discuss the results and ways to improve leadership. If the leadership evaluation is ineffective, it is probably time to call in a facilitator, a neutral third party who can assist the board and the chief executive officer in talking through problems and reaching consensus on workable solutions. Facilitation means "an easing" and this is what a skilled facilitator does, helping members of the group feel at ease so they find it possible to discuss difficult matters.

It should be noted here that boards serving

institutions wholly or partially funded by state or other local government are subject to public disclosure laws. This means that any meeting they hold that includes a quorum of board members must be announced in advance and be open to the public. Exceptions to the rule vary from state to state, but common possibilities for meeting privately include personnel matters, real estate purchases, or other matters considered inappropriate for airing in public. In a small number of states the restrictions of public disclosure make it unusually difficult for a board to convene in private. The only legal choice is to air sensitive problems in a public meeting, which in my view is harmful to board processes needed to solve sensitive problems. In a very sensitive case, the board executive committee should work with the CEO and perhaps an attorney to decide whether the situation is so extreme that it should be discussed in a public meeting despite the embarrassment to involved personnel and the organization.

For those interested in studying this subject in depth, many organizations teach various aspects of conflict resolution, including universities and dispute resolution centers affiliated with local governments. The following short bibliography lists classic publications on group process and conflict resolution.

Bibliography

- Doyle, Michael and Strauss, David. *How to Make Meetings Work: The New Interaction Method.* New York: JovePublications, 1982.

- Gray, Barbara. *Collaborating: Finding Common Ground for Multiparty Problems.* San Francisco, CA: Jossey-Bass Publishers, 1989.

- Mink, Oscar G, Owen, Keith Q. and Mink, Barbara P. *Developing High-Performance People, The Art of Coaching.* Reading, MA: Addison-Wesley Publishing Company, 1993.

- Schwartz, Roger M. *The Skilled Facilitator: Practical Wisdom for Developing Effective Groups.* San Francisco, CA: Jossey-Bass Publishers, 1994.

- Senge, Peter M. *The Fifth Discipline: The Art and Practice of the Learning Organization.* New York: Doubleday / Currency, 1994

**Talking
the Board Talk**

Notes

_____

_____

_____

_____

_____

_____

_____

_____

_____

_____

_____

_____

_____

_____

_____

_____

_____

_____

_____

_____

Commitment

CEO's Commitment

Board Members' Commitment

Troubled leadership in the governance of nonprofits can stem from a lack of commitment on the part of one or more individuals, whether CEO or board member. How can this be? CEO's should be chosen through careful screening and thorough interviews. We've talked about important ways to select good board members. For the most part, these processes work well. The outcome is a leadership team committed to the mission and vision of the organization, and to following the dictates of policies developed by their boards.

But some people do slip through the cracks. The

concern is how to ensure that all members of the leadership team share an appropriate commitment to the institution, a determination that moves the enterprise forward in the best interests of clients and community.

CEO's Commitment

In the case of CEOs who are out of sync with their boards, the problem may be not so much a lack of commitment, but the wrong kind of commitment. I've seen early in an executive's tenure, during what should be a honeymoon time when the board and CEO are learning to work with one another, such a separation between the two that the new leader lasted less than six months. Why? The CEO had a vision for a large, important institution that didn't match the board's perspective, which was not revealed during the hiring process. There was a failure somewhere along the line of the process used to select, hire, and provide board guidance to the new CEO. It was a costly and embarrassing mistake. The obvious lesson is that boards need to take their CEO hiring procedures very seriously, assuring that the new leader is in fact an excellent fit for the organization.

There can also be *too much commitment.* I worked with a nonprofit board led by an attorney who had a vision for an art organization that would have a wonderful building on a prize piece of property, donated by another non-profit organization in the community. The attorney, a sincere fellow with a great vision, acted as executive director. The mission statement and vision were excellent. Good policies were developed. A board of fine community members had been recruited and on the surface was functioning well. But after a couple of years the organization collapsed and the donated land was returned to the donor. What went wrong?

The attorney was so involved with his vision that he took action on almost every responsibility of board and management. There was not enough delegation of tasks. Committed board members need to be active in more ways than sitting around at board meetings listening to what others have done.

And the lesson is clear: finding a CEO who is appropriately committed to the new organization, its mission and policies, is all-important for success.

Board Member's Commitment

In my experience, commitment problems are more common with individual board members than with CEO's. Board members should be people who share a commitment to the institution served.

It's important to think here about the wide range of nonprofits. There are social service agencies serving the poor and hungry or giving shelter to the homeless; tax-exempt organizations supporting symphony orchestras and little-theater groups; nonprofit institutions such as community hospitals and educational institutions. Each of these organizations deserves a board made up of individuals with an interest and belief in the work done by the organization served, and a dedication to the mission set forth by the board.

That's a nice ideal I've just put forward, but as with most ideals it's not always found to be true in the real world. In practice, there are some people who have agendas that differ from the boards they seek to join, with reasons ranging from frivolous to serious. The first could be a social climber wanting to get closer to board members seen as being on a rung or two higher on the social ladder. Those with serious agendas can be more dangerous, especially if they are planning to use membership on the board as a way of advancing a political career. The risk they pose for a board is that they are typically clever talkers and well-versed in board work, giving them the ability to change board vision or paralyze board work. It happens.

Fortunately, those cases are rare. As with other human activities, there are some boards that function exceptionally well, some that do an efficient job, and only a few at the other end. The cliché "singing out of the same songbook" describes a good majority of boards that support the policies and vision set by their past and present directors. If your board is singing out of tune it's time for some self-assessment that includes identifying failures in commitment and ways to correct them.

Notes

_____

_____

_____

_____

_____

_____

_____

Commitment

_____

_____

_____

_____

_____

_____

_____

Notes

_____

_____

_____

_____

_____

_____

_____

_____

_____

_____

_____

_____

_____

_____

_____

_____

_____

_____

_____

_____

_____

Advocacy and Fundraising

In working with a variety of boards through the years, I've found that interest in advocating for their institutions has not been a high priority among board members. Yet the subject of advocacy merits serious thought.

In the earlier discussion of board duties I listed fiscal responsibility along with others, including oversight of revenues and spending. This book is written during a time of serious economic downturn, which has brought strain for most nonprofit organizations. Government-supported nonprofits suffer from a drying up of public monies, while organizations dependent solely on fund-raising find that many of their revenue sources are no longer able to give as they have in the past.

What part should board members play in raising

funds for their institutions? There could be many different answers to the question, depending on the type of organization and its financial underpinnings. There are foundations that have endowments valued at millions or even billions of dollars, and small agencies struggling to pay the electric bills for their offices. Despite those variations, I have one answer for all nonprofit board members: Advocacy.

No matter how you have been chosen as a board member—elected, appointed or by board peers—you are a person of the community with a stake in the success of the institution your board serves. It follows that your interest in the organization makes you better informed than the average community member and you will become even more informed during your tenure as a board member. So what do you do with all that good information? My concern is that most nonprofit board members don't do much beyond telling family and friends about the fine work their organization does for the community.

Advocacy for Funding

Most of us don't have the advantage enjoyed by a few huge foundations, where it would seem that stewardship of rich endowments is more important than fund-raising. The majority of nonprofits are dependent on consistent efforts for monetary support, together with an occasional fundraising campaign. Some that have government funding look for additional support from their communities, and others are wholly funded by community support.

Most of the boards and their members I have known tend to be focused on advocacy that is clearly targeted at their major funding sources. This focus is certainly important to the financial health of their organizations. And it is much more fun and exciting to travel to a state capitol for talks with legislators, to meet with a county executive, or have lunch in the executive dining room of a major corporation, than it is to ask ordinary citizens for financial support.

According to *Giving USA,* total charitable giving in the U.S. reached more than $300 billion dollars in 2008 and $303 billion in 2009. Of that amount 75 percent came from individuals. Funding strategies can be complicated and unique to nonprofits with various needs, but it's easy to conclude that board members should pay attention to approaching individuals in their communities. Asking potential donors for money is a scary proposition for many board members. If a nonprofit is lucky enough to have a development office or single staff member skilled in fundraising, help in overcoming that concern may come from such a source. Otherwise, the nonprofit board should seek training for its members from organizations

Advocacy

offering assistance in fundraising for local nonprofit organizations.

There is one all-important matter of board support for fundraising that is too often overlooked: 100 percent giving by all board members. It's puzzling why this is true, since a proper approach asks the members to give to the best of their ability, even if they can give only a few dollars. I think those who are reluctant to donate are either embarrassed by not being able to give a large amount, or they fear their gift will be compared openly with those of fellow board members who are better off financially. Whoever administers this area of fundraising should make sure that details of the donations are held strictly confidential, to reassure board members. Whatever amount they donate personally, board members should be able to say with pride that they are part of a board of directors having members who all give to the organization.

Advocacy in the Community

Over the last quarter century a couple of fundraising activities have been developed that are so popular that they have become competitive as a result. I'm thinking of auctions and golf tournaments. It's difficult to maintain an even playing field for nonprofits with fewer resources than the large organizations, but from my observation the activities have settled into appropriately larger and smaller affairs that fit the particular nonprofits' resources.

A significant part of nonprofit golf tournaments and auctions in addition to raising funds is "friend-raising." They're wonderful ways of introducing community members to the nonprofits and their importance to the community. They can help to reach that 75 percent of the donor base so important to supporting nonprofit institutions. And they can help generate enthusiasm of board members, capturing their interest and increasing the kind of teamwork so necessary for good governance.

There's another side of advocacy that I find more difficult when trying to enthuse board members, probably due in part to the results being harder to see. This is a marketing approach, making an effort to reach the widest number of local citizens with information about the organization represented. Some larger organizations have marketing departments, and it's too easy to leave that responsibility to them. People who staff these departments know tricks of the marketing trade, but they do not have what board members have.

What board members have is what attracted them to serve as board members: spirit. Spirit comes from a deep knowledge of the organization and personal commitment to its mission. Spirit comes from caring about our community and wanting to make it better. This

Advocacy

may seem like a nebulous characteristic for advantage in promoting a nonprofit institution, but I believe it exists and can be understood by carefully observing board members who have that advantage, who have that spirit.

What can board members do to help market their institutions? One answer could be to write an opinion piece for the editorial page in your local newspaper. Do you belong to a fraternal organization or similar group? These people are often looking for speakers at their meetings, a great opportunity to tell your nonprofit story. If you don't consider yourself a speaker, chances are that your organization has a video you could show to your friends at clubs, churches and other places community people get together.

Finally, in my opinion the best presentation of this type is a committed board member who is a good public speaker, together with a client who is able to tell a compelling story of how he or she has been benefited by the nonprofit. Listeners who come to hear this kind of presentation often are thinking about their pocketbooks in closed position as they enter, and think more openly when hit by an emotional presentation.

Afterword

A reader might conclude from what I've written that there are a lot of poorly managed nonprofit boards out there. I don't want to close leaving you with that opinion. Most nonprofit boards are doing a good job of governing organizations that contribute significantly to the health, welfare, education and other life-needs in communities ranging from remote hamlets to our largest cities.

I've described poorly run boards and given anecdotes about questionable board member behavior (including my own). I hope that what readers will take away from this book are some ideas to help their nonprofit boards manage governance well, and in the process, help their board members get more enjoyment out of the process.

Soon after ACCT began marketing *Essentials of Good*

Board/CEO Relations to their members, I attended one of their national conferences. Following a workshop a trustee approached me with great praise for the book. She went on at length about how much she liked it, so much so that she had just purchased six copies to distribute to her fellow board members.

"What was it that you liked so much about the book?" I asked.

"I liked it because it was so short," she said, adding "I was able to read the whole book on the airplane flight back home." (She lived only a few hundred miles away from where she bought the first copy.)

That experience was high in my mind as I wrote this book, keeping it short for the busy people who volunteer for nonprofit boards. I hope they will gain insight by reading this, and that it might help their board processes become more efficient and enjoyable.

> *Vaughn A. Sherman*
> *October, 2011*

Readers who would like to connect with the author may contact him by sending an e-mail to *Vaughn@patosislandpress.com*.

Appendix A

SAMPLE

*For Those Considering Membership
on the XYZ Agency Board*

Greetings, and thank you for considering membership on the XYZ Agency Board of Directors. We're pleased that this may be of interest to you, and believe that you would be a fine addition to our Board. Before accepting this position, it's important that you understand the roles and responsibilities of our board members in supporting this institution. An overview of support includes sharing of one's time, talent and treasure.

A first expectation of our Board members is that they have a strong commitment to the XYZ Agency and its mission. You will be part of a team that advocates for and promotes the Agency in the community.

Sharing your time includes several activities:

- Participation in a new board member orientation
- Attending scheduled board meetings, about _____ hours per month
- Attending retreats, held _____ (annually, semi-annually, etc.)
- Serving on committees, about _____ hours per month
- Attending Agency special events such as receptions

There is an expectation that members will give priority to attending board meetings, and that they will miss no more than three monthly meetings a year. Members are asked to notify the leadership a week in advance when unable to attend a meeting.

The talent you bring to the board will be unique to a group made up of unique individuals, each bringing his or her own skills and experience. An important part of our board philosophy is that it be made up of individuals who bring diverse perspectives to our deliberations, people whose experiences enrich the board's governance and the institution itself.

We ask that board members contribute to the board's annual donation drive each year. Members are asked to donate to the best of their ability. (Alternatively: Each board member is asked to donate or raise a minimum of _____ each year. This may take the form of a personal donation, bringing in sponsors for events, and other means of raising revenue.)

Board members can expect to be rewarded with the knowledge that they have made a positive contribution to the continued success and growth of the institution. Many board members comment on the personal growth they have experienced, and the friendships developed through service to the board.

Notes

_____

_____

_____

_____

_____

_____

_____

_____

_____

_____

_____

_____

_____

_____

_____

_____

_____

_____

_____

_____

_____

Appendix B

Chief Executive Officer Evaluation

There are several matters to consider when fashioning an evaluation of a chief executive officer:

- Goals for the evaluation. Most often the board wants an opportunity to reach agreement on the executive director's performance during the past year. This is also a time to determine how the CEO views his or her own performance, and an opportunity to assist this leader in improving the performance when needed.

- The format for the evaluation should be based on discussions between the board and CEO, and agreed to by all before being used.

- The focus should be on the CEO's job description. The board should not evaluate a CEO duty that he or she was clearly not asked to perform in the job description or documented delegation of duties.
- A decision should be made as to whether or not constituents should be involved in the evaluation.
- The process should allow sufficient time for discussion of the evaluation between the CEO and the board.
- The board must be honest throughout its approach to the evaluation. Avoid inflating or deflating the evaluation as a means of manipulating the CEO's relationship with the board.
- Reporting on evaluation conclusions should again be based on mutual agreement between CEO and board. Should there be a written report for the personnel file? Shoud the public be made aware of the findings in a report given at a regular meeting of the board?

Many, many examples of CEO evaluation instruments float around nonprofit circles, most of them excellent—as applied to the particular institution for which they were written. The spread of governance models, even within the same service area of agencies, is so broad that each board should write its own evaluation instrument for and with the CEO. That's not to say that model instruments should not be reviewed; rather, review them and tailor what they have developed to fit your institution.

Here are a few of the points covered in several examples of CEO evaluations resting in my files:

(The CEO . . .)

» **Board Relations**

- Regularly and adequately informs the board about operations and activities of the organization and is responsive to information requests from the board.
- Is responsive and appropriate in carrying out directions from the board.
- Maintains honest and open relations with the board. Communication with board members is even-handed, with no favoritism shown to individual members beyond the special relationship with the board chair.

» **Campus and Community Relationships**

- Regularly attends community events and is known to support programs that are organized by the institution.
- Has a thorough knowledge of all the organization's programs and activities.
- Actively participates in community activities and takes leadership roles as appropriate.

Appendices

- Is active in local, state and national associations representing the organization's areas of interest, at a level consistent with needs of the organization.

Financial Concerns

- Has an excellent understanding of fiscal matters as applied to this organization's area of service.
- Oversees preparation of budgets that are realistic and supportive of the mission. Sufficient time is spent in financial discussions with the board that all directors are able to understand budgets and financial underpinnings.
- Maintains fiscal support of the organization as a primary goal and acts as a leader in securing funding.
- Regularly reports to the board on financial matters, and alerts the board immediately to concerns about the organization's financial health.

» Programs

- Understands and implements the mission and goals set forth by the board.
- Delivers services that are responsive and innovative with regard to the community's changing needs.
- Understands and appropriately responds to the needs of clients and the community.

This small sampling barely touches the broad range of topics used by nonprofit boards in evaluations of executive directors. I use it here in the hope that it might jumpstart a board's discussions about evaluating their CEO, keeping in mind that the evaluation must reflect the particular assessment needs of the board, the CEO and the organization itself.

Appendices

Notes

Appendix C

Board Self-Evaluation

In comparing board self-evaluation instruments against those used for evaluating executive directors, there appears to be a greater commonality among the instruments for board self-evaluations across the various lines of service. However, this is not to suggest that designing a self-evaluation instrument for boards is an easier exercise than doing the same for evaluation of a CEO.

It's important to think here about the need for cohesiveness and teamwork for any nonprofit board. A board self-evaluation should be seen in this light, and in terms of the maturity and effectiveness of the board as a whole, not individual board members. Boards wishing to evaluate individual members should use instruments with questions helping members understand how effectively each is contributing to board work. These instruments need to be completed in private, not shared with other board members. However, a well-functioning board may be able to have a conversation about the experience of completing the assessment instrument, with some members willing to share responses helpful to others.

As with evaluation instruments for executive directors, there are a great many examples available in nonprofit circles. One resource offers ten topics and more than 100 questions for selection in building an instrument. Following is an abbreviated selection of topics and questions in an excellent board evaluation instrument in my files:

» **Institutional Mission Policy**
  - The Board has a clear understanding of the mission
  - The Board has a clear understanding of policies and reviews them regularly.
  - The Board demonstrates leadership in development of policies and links them to its decision-making.

» **Planning**
  - The Board includes contributions from constituents and various interest groups in its planning.
  - The Board is an active leader in development of

institutional goals.

- Planning is considered a vital part of the Board's responsibilities to the institution.

» Financial Resources

- The Board shows leadership in securing financial support for the organization
- The Board accepts and exercises its responsibility for fiscal oversight.
- The Board carefully reviews and approves the budget.

» Board Organization

- Board meetings are conducted in accordance with policy governing meeting rules.
- Members demonstrate that they have studied the agenda prior to the meeting
- Time at Board meetings is used effectively for discussion of agenda items.

» Board/President Relations

- The Board has clearly designated the authority under which the CEO manages the institution.
- The Board and CEO have a clear understanding of established channels of communication with faculty, staff and students.
- A climate of mutual trust and support exists between the Board and executive director

» **Scoring**

There are many scoring methods used for evaluation instruments, from *Satisfactory / Unsatisfactory / No Opinion* to a numbering system from *0* for neutral to *1* for low and *5* for high; to many other variations. It's recommended that a board use a system common in the institution, or if it's a small organization just pick a system and stick to it when using evaluation or similar instruments.

It's hoped that these few topics and questions will be found useful as a beginning framework for a nonprofit board to build a more complete self-evaluation, one that reflects the governing interests and needs of the board and its individual members.

Wise governance provides its leaders time to regularly consider and improve the effectiveness of its efforts on behalf of the governed. Every nonprofit governing board, no matter its size, needs to keep this in mind.

Author's Notes

My sincere thanks to many who helped me with this project, some old friends and some newer, but all helpful beyond my expectations.

Jennifer McCord, of Jennifer McCord Associates LLC, is a highly professional book consultant who guided me on the road to forming Patos Island Press LLC, a boutique publishing firm. She has also been instrumental as a consultant in publishing this book, the first release from Patos Island Press. Two additional books are in preparation for release in 2012, one the memoir of a northwest mariner, and the other a children's book written by my wife and business partner, Jan Lind-Sherman.

Others who were key to publishing *Walking the Board Walk* include editor Sheryl Stebbins; and Jeanie

James, who did the layout and design. I enjoyed the benefit of their talents and found them great to work with.

The colleagues who provided opening remarks about the book deserve special attention. I think it's fair to say that during our many years of working together we have shared with each other, learned from each other, and have been blessed with opportunities to grow through involvement with education and philanthropy at several levels. Their patient review of a couple of drafts of this book and resulting suggestions were key to its completion, and deeply appreciated. Here are more details about them.

Dr. Cindra Smith has conducted close to 200 workshops for more than 80 community college governing boards and leadership teams. Retired as Director of Education Service for the Community College League of California, she is now an independent consultant with focuses on facilitation, board development, goal setting, professional development, evaluation, and teaching. In addition to her work with the League, she has been a Special Consultant for Trustee Education for the Association of Community College Trustees. She has also taught in the Community College Faculty Preparation Certificate program offered at California State University, Sacramento. Dr. Smith is the author of *Trusteeship in Community Colleges: A Guide to Effective Governance* (2000).

Gary Davis earned a PhD from the University of Iowa before being promoted to professor and department chair at Northwest Missouri State University. He served as Assistant to the President and Secretary to the Board of Control at Saginaw State University. He was CEO of the Illinois Community College Trustees Association and served as a board retreat facilitator for the Association of Community College Trustees and the Association of Governing Boards. His articles on trusteeship are published by ACCT and Jossey-Bass. Dr. Davis is the owner of Board Solutions, and has conducted more than 200 retreats nationally.

Chris Marx is the Executive Director of the Edmonds Community College Foundation located in Lynnwood, Washington. She has served in the nonprofit sector for fifteen years, with a professional background in fundraising, administration, program management and public relations. Marx holds a Masters in Public Administration, Bachelor's degree, and certificate in non-profit management, all from the University of Washington.

Readers are invited to contact me at *Vaughn@ patosislandpress.com.*

About the Author

Vaughn Sherman

Vaughn Sherman was born and raised in the Seattle area, where he attended Roosevelt High School and the University of Washington. His first career was as a fisheries biologist, working in Washington State and Alaska. Following that he spent more than twenty years as an operations officer with the Central Intelligence Agency, most of the time on assignments abroad.

After retirement Vaughn was launched on a variety of community activities, many involved with the governance of nonprofit agencies and community colleges. United Way of Snohomish County included him in a Boardwalk Program that prepared volunteers as trainers for boards of United Way agencies. Through training sessions and retreat leadership he has helped many Snohomish County agencies with governance matters.

Vaughn has been deeply involved with community college education, beginning with a 1981 appointment as a trustee for Edmonds Community College. Since then he has served as President of Washington State's Trustees Association of Community and Technical Colleges (TACTC), and President of the national Association of Community College Trustees (ACCT). He is a consultant for ACCT, and has made presentations and led retreats for community college boards in all corners of the country.

As noted in this book he has written several articles and two small books for ACCT and other community college organizations. He has also authored a novel based on his CIA career, *Sasha Plotkin's Deceit,* which will be released by Coffee Town Press in early summer 2012. His *Memoir of a Master Mariner* will be released by Patos Island Press about the same time.

Vaughn served fifteen years as an Edmonds Community College trustee, and as a Director of the Washington State Community College Foundation for another fifteen years. A certified mediator, he is a volunteer with the Dispute Resolution Center of Snohomish, Island Counties and Skagit Counties. He lives in Edmonds with his wife, Jan Lind-Sherman, and with her enjoys a large family spread throughout the Pacific Northwest.

Notes

Notes

Notes

Notes

www.patosislandpress.com